the episcopal
call to love

by rob gieselmann

the apocryphile press
BERKELEY, CA
www.apocryphile.org

apocryphile press
BERKELEY, CA

Apocryphile Press
1700 Shattuck Ave #81
Berkeley, CA 94709
www.apocryphile.org

Printed in the United States of America
ISBN 1-933993-60-X

contents

chapter one
erred and strayed

The Problem: Collective Sin

This is the book nobody will like.

The Episcopal Church has gone crazy. We've become pigs who roll around in our own mud, and when we've finished rolling here, we roll there. Perhaps we eat a little spiritual food and then wallow back to the mud. We talk about God, mention Jesus like he's our best friend, but we act exactly like he said not to act. *We are* exactly who he said *not to be*.

We're trying, so we say. We're trying to work through the present rift. If *talking* is any indication, we're trying hard. If *analyzing* is any indication, we're trying even harder. *The Eames Commission, The Windsor Report, The Living Church*, loads of blogs and too many websites to count. Who is David Virtue, anyway?

The bishops have conferenced and retreated *ad nauseam.* Canterbury. New York. Kanuga. Texas. Worse, our bishops, united by *apostolic authority and succession,* have themselves become divided by intransigence, political maneuvering, and anger.

Not to mention the Anglican Communion. As the word "communion" suggests, we, the Episcopal Church, are in this with others; we are mired in mud with Anglicans the world over. Nigerian archbishops refuse to take communion with American presiding bishops, Rwandan bishops ordain men extraterritorially to serve as priests in the United States, Canadian churches approve rites for same sex unions over the objection of the rest, and Ugandans reject vital welfare hard-earned and offered with love.

The earth is quaking, and one might, if one squinted and looked to the eastern horizon, imagine Jesus on a cloud descending, coming again to judge the quick, if not the dead. Us. Both quick and dead.

For we have sinned, and there is no health in us. Community Sin, for which community atonement must be made.

Make no mistake about it. Our very division is sin, perhaps even with a capital "S". Mortal sin. As in the death of a church, a death that is both unnecessary and un-Christian; it is altogether un-Christ-like.

The Blame

Perhaps like the petulant child you blame someone else and declare—*His fault; not mine. I did right.*

Stayed faithful. But, of-course, you'd be wrong. I don't care how *right*eous you are in this whole thing, or should I say, *how righteous you think you are*, this division is our fault, the fault of the whole. If we are a conservative evangelical, the fault is ours. If we are a liberal Anglican, the fault is ours. If we are an African bishop or a gay parishioner, the fault is ours. If we are Rowan Williams, the fault is ours. It's called *collective fault*, as in collective sin, as in **we** *confess that* **we** *have sinned against you, in thought, word and deed, by what* **we** *have done, and by what* **we** *have left undone.* Your sin is my sin, and mine yours. Jesus had a lot to say about collective sin—or should I say, he had a lot to do about collective sin.

Collective sin. Just like good-ole-Israel. The Book of Chronicles calls *all of Israel* to repentance. The deeds of some are attributed to the whole.

Likewise, with bony finger raised in Israel's face, John the Baptist called the entire nation to repentance, not just individuals. *You brood of vipers,* he said to the crowds *as one.* (Lk. 3:7) *Who told you to flee from the wrath to come?* To those more concerned about their own form of apostolic succession, John added this invective: *Don't you know, God is able to raise up sons of Abraham from these stones!* (Lk. 3:8).

Jesus, too, called the nation of Israel to repentance, not just individuals (see generally, Mark 11). He wept over Jerusalem as a mother over its chicks—not individuals, but the whole. The barren fig tree withered at Jesus' curse. The fig tree represents Israel, and not just one lazy person. The vineyard entrusted to Israel was recovered by God the landowner, who installed other tenants. Indeed, Jesus' very presence in Jerusalem and his immediate pilgrimage to the Temple when he came to town was his declaration by action that he intended fully to recover the worship for a people who would *actually* worship—be they Jew or Gentile.

Scripture is replete with instances in which God calls groups to repentance, and not just individuals. Self-righteous groups, groups who think they have God on their side, are shocked to discover God on the other side.

Surely you remember the fellow Jesus talked about, the one who imagined he had no sin, and stood before God as one innocent? *Thank you, God, I'm not like that poor sinner over there!* I've heard lots of posturing over the past three and one-half years that sounds quite a bit like that foolish guy: *I'm glad I have an in with you, God, unlike those poor folks over there.* All "sides."

The Scriptural literalists imagine Scripture will save them. But it was Jesus, and not Scripture, who died.

The progressives imagine their inclusiveness will save them. But it was Jesus, and not social engineering, who died.

Meanwhile, that poor sinner is on his knees over there beating his chest, *God have mercy on me, a sinner.* Jesus is still asking, *which of the two walked away forgiven?*

I notice that the *Prayer of Humble Access* has fallen into disfavor these days. I'm guessing it has fallen out of favor because it begins with these words: *We do not presume to come to this thy table, O merciful Lord....* We don't like the prayer exactly because we *do* presume, week after week, to come to this God's table. We presume, despite the patent sin of our division, without apology, without repentance.

Some people posit that it is better for the church to split.[1] Is split so bad? Indeed, beyond some point, permanent split may become inevitable. But split is seldom, if ever, God's plan. Unity and loyalty always exist on a higher plane than division. Paul was quite succinct and quite angry when addressing the divisive Corinthians: *Can Christ be divided*? The Lord's Prayer is a unity prayer, a church prayer, and belongs to no one but the whole. The unified whole. Not the half over here, or the half over there.

Where is Collective Love?

I told you that you wouldn't like this little book. And you will like this statement even less: Only a few seem to be trying very hard to find out what God wants, what the Holy Spirit is saying, or, to use the pop phrase, WWJD? Indeed, *What would Jesus do?* I'm guessing here, but I imagine Jesus in Moses fashion would—were it possible—take the two tablets inscribed with the Sermon on the Mount, and throw them against the ground, grinding them into dust. Leaving the shards behind, Jesus would return to the

Temple in Jerusalem, where he would upend the tables of our property arguments (*really, now,* who owns the churches anyway?).

I have a little child's book called *If Jesus Came to my House,* by Joan Gale Thomas (Lothrop, Lee & Shepard, 1951), given to me as a child. Listening to simple meter and verse, one imagines how good one might act if Jesus came for a child's play date visit. The plot-twist comes at the end of the book. Jesus visits, but only in the form of the *Other*. The other person, the one with whom you so vehemently disagree. How do you treat that person?

> *And I can make Him welcome*
> *as He Himself has said,*
> *by doing all I would for Him*
> *for other folk instead.*

Collective love is the only way forward.

We Have Sinned, and There Is No Health in Us

You might defend your actions by noting how harshly Jesus spoke to the religious leaders who imagined they owned the truth. But, let's be clear: you aren't Jesus. What gives you the right to claim truth? And worse, if you listen closely, you might hear in your own voice echoes of the same religious leaders Jesus excoriated.

It is time for each of us to stop sounding like we own the truth. And just so you will know, as I so arrogantly write these sentences, I fall to my knees (at this moment, I bow my knee, even as I write), and ask for forgiveness, and God's grace, and for the truth of Christ to emerge despite my cold heart.

Some of you will say, when a human right is at stake, stake a claim. I've heard that argument, and I've heard the comparison to slavery and civil rights. First of all, not all homosexual behavior is about human right. Indeed, I'm still waiting for apologists to stop lumping all homosexuality into the same pail, as though all homosexual activity[2] is acceptable. At the least, we can and should agree that some homosexual activity is patently unacceptable, just like some heterosexual activity is patently unacceptable.

To be sure, a human right may be at stake, and if so, a claim is worth staking. However, I'm looking for those who will promote the cause like Abraham Lincoln promoted freedom to slaves. He agonized over the division of the Union. He prayed passionately before issuing the Emancipation Proclamation, and he genuinely lamented the fracture of the Union and absolved the South at the end of it all.

To the homosexuals among us I would say, *isn't patience in order?* After all, how long did it take you to come to terms with your own sexuality? Can you reasonably expect heterosexuals to make the transition faster than you did?

Others of you will say sin is sin, and God says homosexual behavior is sin. I've heard that argument, and I've heard that God won't bless the Church that condones egregious sin. Okay. Why is it, then, that we don't talk about more popular forms of sin: cheating on taxes, adultery, fornication, or—watch out, here—keeping holy the Sabbath?[3] *Even if* you are right, and all homosexual behavior is sin (a discussion worth continuing for many reasons, but not here), the issue shouldn't split the church, unless you're ready for the Church to split over these other issues, as well. I'm looking for honesty among the more conservative among us, an admission that, for the most part, Scripture is being manipulated to hide prejudice—plain, good, old-fashioned prejudice (a.k.a. homophobia). It is time to own it.

The Cross of Christ: Faith

The cross of Christ points in two directions, not just one. Jesus' arms are wide enough for a complex of individuals and spiritualities to coexist. But we treat the cross as though it points in one direction only, ours.

Which leads me to this question: why is it we don't trust Jesus as the Christ, along with the benefactor Holy Spirit, to guide us through this? To seek God's will? (Seeking God's will means you come to the priedieu, hands extended, palms facing upward, without the answer, without presupposition.) Are we so afraid of what God might say that we refuse to listen?

We call ourselves *believers*, but we don't believe. We call ourselves *lovers*, but we love only those who love us in return. We call ourselves the *saved*, but we are a people lost to conflict.

Sadly, the world itself is mired in reproachable conflict. Not just military or international conflict, but internal conflict. Oh, the things we do and say to one another. This world longs as a mother in childbirth for a better way, the way that Jesus taught and we, as the church should be offering. But we aren't offering, bickering instead like puerile children, dividing over issues that shouldn't divide, pretending that Jesus didn't die for all of us, didn't rise again to defeat the very evil in which we find ourselves mired. The evil of division.

It is time to seek God's forgiveness, and move forward in Christ. To proclaim the Gospel, the Good News, and to live it, as well.

Shouldn't we turn, turn from our petty sin and selfishness, and forge a better way forward? Indeed we should. Indeed we must.

Introductory Notes

Several close friends have suggested that the rhetoric in this first chapter is far too strident, that the volume of my complaint will prevent you from hearing the message. I reminded my friends that our heritage is replete with stridency—both Paul and Jesus are strident when necessary. They smiled and reminded me that I am, of-course, neither Paul nor Jesus. (To quote myself, what gives me the right to claim truth?) I am but a simple priest serving in a small Northern California parish.

All of this is to say, I considered rewriting this chapter. But I couldn't. These words, however terse, are the words I find in my heart. I am disturbed over our pettiness, and I'm pretty sure most middle-of-the-road Episcopal Christians are, too. We are divided unnecessarily, and it is time to reunite. For this reason, I hope you will both indulge and forgive me, and continue reading.

In the chapters that follow, I will employ Scripture to demonstrate that both Jesus and Paul would favor unity over division, and that the Holy Eucharist is the ultimate act of Christian unity. I hope to show that, in the end, unity in Christ should be our goal, not righteousness. Division may be our destiny, but it is not God's will.

Finally, I am addressing conflict in the Episcopal Church, not in the Anglican Communion. What I write about the Episcopal Church likely applies to the Anglican Communion. The irony of the present conflict is that those exercising majority power in the Episcopal Church—the progressives—find themselves in the minority in the Anglican Communion. Those exercising power in the Anglican Communion are conservative—people like Nigerian Bishop Akinola, and American Marty Minns.[4] Roles are reversed, but the practical theology needed is same. Repentance for division. Love. Laying down of preconceived notions. Ceasing all shenanigans. Yielding, and trusting. Trusting Jesus.

chapter two
the more excellent way

The Corinthians did not love. That was their collective sin. Love, wrote Paul in his most beautiful prose, is kind. Love is *always* patient—always patient and kind. It is not boastful, does not demand its own way, does not rejoice when others do it wrong, but is always ready to excuse, to trust, to hope, and to endure whatever may come. Love is always patient and kind (1 Cor. 13:4-6).

Paul wrote these words to a church mired in conflict like we Episcopalians, pigs in mud. And Paul was hopping mad. This church was one he had formed, these people were his, those he cared about, birthed as babies to be Christians. Paul had been their midwife, their wet-nurse. He nursed them even as a mother her baby. He taught them better than this; and he left them in trust, one to another, a trust they breached.

Corinth and the Corinthian Church

Originally a Greek city, Corinth was destroyed by the Romans in 146 BCE. Julius Caesar restored Corinth in 44 BCE, and by the time Paul visited, Corinth was the capital of Achia. Strategically located along the main trade route across an isthmus between the Aegean and Adriatic seas, Corinth was also flanked by two ports, one in each sea. Corinth thus enjoyed trade access to both water and land, and it was wealthy. Finally, Corinth hosted Olympic games and was integral to the regional culture.

In short, Corinth was a major political, business, and social center through which diverse people regularly passed. The Corinthian church reflected this diversity, and included members who were wealthy and poor (1 Cor. 1:26), male and female, of high social standing and of lower social standing, slave and free (1 Cor. 7:21), married and unmarried (1 Cor. 7:27), Jew and Gentile.

Paul traveled to Corinth in approximately 50 CE, while on what has become known as his Second Missionary Journey (Acts 18:2). He founded the Corinthian Church the same way he founded other churches. When entering Corinth, he went immediately to the Corinthian Synagogue and preached the Gospel to the Jews there (Acts 18:4). By this time in his ministry, Paul welcomed the Greeks without hesitation, so when many of the Jews rejected the Good News that Jesus is the Christ, Paul shook his cloak as a sign of discontinuity and breach, turning instead to the *pagans*, the Gentiles (Acts 18:6).

Paul believed that he had built the Corinthian church on the one sure foundation of Jesus Christ (1 Cor. 3:10-11), and Christ crucified (1 Cor. 2:2). He did not preach human wisdom; he spoke and demonstrated the power of God (1 Cor. 2:4-5). In short, Paul preached the *kerygmatic*, life-changing, razor's edge message that he taught to other Gentiles, *by grace you are saved, through faith*[5] (Eph. 2:8). Not law, but faith, for *the law of the Spirit of life in Christ Jesus has set you free from the law of sin and death*, Paul wrote to the Church at Rome (Rom. 8:2).

You are not under the law, but grace (Rom. 6:14). Paul was so convinced that remaining under the law would yield only death, that he wrote a terse letter to the church at Galatia warning them against subjecting themselves a second time to the law. *Stand firm*, Paul wrote, *and do not submit again to a yoke of slavery* (Gal. 5:2).

The Corinthians had heard a similar message, perhaps from Paul himself, or from Apollos. Some became confused because of conflicting instructions, for example, *It is well for a man not to touch a woman* (1 Cor. 7:1), and *all things are lawful* (1 Cor. 6:12). When he wrote similar words to the Romans, Paul anticipated their next question: *Should we continue in sin in order that grace might abound?* (Rom. 6:1). To Paul's dismay, the Corinthians would have answered, *yes*, to this question. Their lifestyles implicated them of an unholy liberty, which Paul addressed in this letter to them. The Corinthians obviously misunderstood the liberty offered in the *kerygmatic* message of the Gospel, with its natural fruit being the desire to please God, not the liberty to sin.

The Corinthian Division

After Paul left Corinth, other evangelists arrived, including Apollos. Apollos was a Jew that Paul had met in Ephesus. He was eloquent and knowledgeable of both Scripture and Jesus, but he had received only John's baptism. Paul's friends, Priscilla and Aquila, took Apollos aside and instructed him more deeply in *the Way*. It is unclear whether Apollos ever received the Holy Spirit like the early followers, although it appears that others in the same situation did (Acts 18:24-28).

Later, this eloquent and charismatic preacher traveled to Corinth after Paul, and taught the Corinthians. Was Apollos' message somehow different from Paul's, or was his persona so inviting that members of the church began to identify more closely with him than with Paul? Or, perhaps, did the Corinthians confuse the messenger with the message? *I am for Paul*, some declared. *I am for Apollos,* or *I am for Cephas*. Paul mocked the litany of diverse loyalties in the opening to his letter by declaring emphatically, *I am for Christ.*

I am for Christ. Which is, of-course, the same message of loyalty we proclaim: *In Christ there is no*

East nor West, in Him no North or South. And again, *in Christ, our sad divisions cease.* We proclaim, but we, like the Corinthians, can't seem to live together. I am for Scripture; I am for inclusiveness. I am for Gene Robinson. I am against homosexuality. No, *I am for Christ!*

But it wasn't just that some members aligned themselves with Apollos while others aligned themselves with Paul. Their divisions were, as are ours, much deeper.

Because of its trade, Corinthians enjoyed wealth—or, at least some of them enjoyed wealth. Even members of the church were wealthy. Paul opened his letter noting that many members are *not* powerful, wise, or wellborn (1 Cor. 1:26). As Gerd Theissen has noted, the converse must have been true: some were among society's elite.[6]

Likely, members brought their own food to community gatherings. The wealth and social standing of some members meant they could afford to bring meat, but the poor could not. The poor might have eaten meat on rare occasions, which would not have included church gatherings (Theissen, p. 128-29). In fact, the poor would have known of meat only as an ingredient in pagan religious celebrations—and some would have been quite offended to watch the rich eat meat at community gatherings.

But the rich, who had more leisure time to contemplate the spiritual life, and thought of themselves as having *gnosis*, special knowledge, would have understood that God no longer forbids eating such meat. *All things are lawful*, they would have retorted to those opposing them. Eating meat would have *become* spiritual for them, an expression of their freedom in Christ.

To Paul, the wealth issue was crucial only in that it became the source of division, such as between the strong *Gnostics*, who appeared more spiritual and thus closer to God, and the underclass, the struggling Christians who could not afford to bring meat to church. In fact, Paul was deeply disturbed over some members leaving the assembly hungry while others left drunk (1 Cor. 11:21).

Paul's Message of Unity:
The Strong Serve the Weak

Paul wanted the church to return to its unified state—a diverse group, centered around Christ—so he took the *strong*, those with *gnosis*, the supposed *free*, to task. In an ironic twist, Paul cogently pointed out that the supposed strong were, in fact, *not*. The supposed spiritual were, in fact, *not*. The strong were the ones not yet ready for solid food because they had not digested the milk, and this was *obvious* to Paul because of their quarrelling (1 Cor. 3:2-3). Paul warned those who thought they had drunk from the spiritual *rock that is Christ*, that they might be the same as some of Moses' Hebrew children, quite displeasing to God (1 Cor. 10:5, 12 Jerusalem Bible).

Paul consistently warned the supposed *strong* throughout his letter: *take care, you who are standing firm, or you may fall* (2 Cor. 10:12, *Revised English Bible*).

The reason Paul addressed the supposed *strong* so stridently is because their sin infected the whole church. They were disruptive. Indeed, they applied Christian principles correctly—we Christians *are* free to eat meat sacrificed to idols—but Paul judged them absurdly wrong. Their superiority divided the Body of Christ—divided Christ—by far the worse sin. You may feel secure, Paul intimated over and over and over again, but unless your security is based upon the foundation of Christ and Christ crucified, you have become the ultimate fool. Your wisdom is foolishness to God, (*see generally* 1 Cor. 1:18-29), and worse, your wisdom is dividing Christ's Church. Through your own wisdom, you have become no more than a *noisy gong or a clanging cymbal* (1 Cor. 13:1). Your knowledge without love has rendered you as nothing (1 Cor. 13:2).

All of this, of-course, echoes Paul's letter to the Philippians, in which he urged the Philippians to be of the same mind that was in Christ Jesus, who, though rightfully equal to God, did not regard that equality as something to be exploited. Do nothing from selfish ambition or conceit, Paul told them, *but in humility regard others as better than yourselves* (Phil. 2:3, 5-6). And so Paul wrote to the Corinthians,

[W]hether you eat or drink, or whatever you do, do everything for the glory of God. Give no offense to Jews or to Greeks or to the church of God, just as I try to please everyone in everything I do, not seeking my own advantage, but that of many, so that they may be saved (1 Cor. 10:31-33).

Paul reminded the Corinthians: you are not the esteemed you think yourselves to be. God chooses the foolish of the world—a.k.a. you—to shame the wise. You are the *common and contemptible* ones God has chosen (1 Cor. 1:27-28, *The Jerusalem Bible*).

Paul wasn't putting the Corinthians down, but bringing them back to the point of beginning, that we are the same in Christ, and that there is no place for self-exaltation in Christ. Self-exaltation, self-righteousness, a sense that, as Paul wrote later, *I have no need of you, my brother* (1 Cor. 12), denudes Christ and the cross of their wisdom and power[7]—all untenable to Paul. As if echoing Jesus' words that the last shall be first, Paul reminded them that one can be wise only if he is first a fool (*compare* Matt. 19:30 *with* 1 Cor. 3:18).

Put simply, the more *spiritual* members of the Corinthian Church did not bother to understand the *less spiritual*. Had they taken the time to listen, to hear the heart, to understand the sensitivities, perhaps—just perhaps—there would have been no division.

Nobody would admit it, but all sides of our present debate involve quadrants of Christians who imagine themselves to be *the spiritual,* and others to be *the less spiritual.* In fact, some evangelical conservatives have said plainly, *they aren't saved.*[8] Liberal Episcopalians arrogantly imagine that the evangelical conservatives just don't get it, that they are too prejudiced to see truth. And neither is listening to the fact that, actually, the superficial issue of homosexuality is really not the issue at all. The issue is something else altogether, and homosexuality is merely the presenting issue.

Paul saw the church as a theocracy. Each of the Corinthians is a member of the Body of Christ, but Christ is the head (Eph. 4:15). The Spirit of Christ is the blood flowing through the body, bringing it life, uniting it. To survive and thrive, each member needs each other member. We are a living organism, with some strange symbiotic interdependence. Unity occurs not when we are all the same, Paul wrote, but when we live as who we are, when each of us humbly treats the other as more important than ourselves, when we esteem the body parts that seem less seemly.

Corinthian and Episcopal Love: I Need You

And so we love. We love one another. It is, as it turns out, that failure to love is the great failing, the great sin, of the Corinthian church. The thirteenth chapter of First Corinthians was not written for weddings. It was not written to describe a romantic love expressed before it has had time to endure, before it has been jostled by bumps in the road. Rather, the thirteenth chapter of First Corinthians was written for a church divided.

Had the Corinthian Christians not been boastful or conceited, had they not taken pleasure in others' sins, had they stood ready to believe all things and hope all things and endure all things, had they not demanded their own way...Paul would not have judged them. But they did not love, and became instead a noisy gong, a clanging cymbal.

Which, of course, is our failing. We don't love. Indeed, at some deep level, we don't see that we are all necessary to the body of Christ—an organic jigsaw puzzle that is only complete when piece next to piece is fitted and working in God's spirit of love. Can the right hand say to the left, *I have no need of you?* Can the conservative evangelical say to progressive, *I have no need of you? Can Christ be divided?* Paul answered this question for the Corinthians, *of course not.* But we are dividing Christ.

Paul elevated the sin of disdain, or arrogance, of considering oneself more spiritual than the others, above all other sins, for disdain is a failure of love. No, Paul did not esteem unity for unity's sake, but for Christ's sake.

The United States formed a republican democracy based on two principles. First, a vote by popular majority establishes our government and elects individuals to lead, and second, the rights and liberties of the individual cannot be altered or abrogated by the popular majority. In some strange symbiosis of philosophy—a marriage, perhaps of Lockean political philosophy with Pauline ecclesiology, Paul's letter to the Corinthians echoes our American system. Or, vice versa.

Corinthians, Paul writes to those exercising their authority and autonomy (though perhaps not a majority), *you may live your choice—all things **are** lawful—but why would you?* All things **are** lawful, but all things most definitely **are not** expedient. *You may exercise your freedom—all things **are** lawful—but why would you?* When you know your exercise will damage the faith of the person sitting in the pew next to you?

To the great majority in the Episcopal Church, Paul writes, *You can approve an openly gay man in a committed relationship to be bishop—all things **are** lawful—but why would you?* Indeed, Scripture as a reflection of and vehicle for the Divine is flexible and not static law, and God is fully accepting of gay persons—*all things **are** lawful—but when you know that doing so will damage the very faith of good minority, why would you?*[9]

And to the minority fleeing the Episcopal Church in hurt and anger and even righteous indignation (regardless of whether warranted), can you, as Paul writes, say to those *parts* you are leaving behind, *I have no need of you?* How dare you say, *I have no need of you?* But that is exactly what you are saying by leaving.

Of course, one cannot reduce the present discord to simple poles of majority and minority camps. Those favoring the majority or remaining in the Episcopal Church include people of all stripes, of varied theologies. Moderates, progressives, disinterested, liberals, liberal evangelicals, iconoclasts, and so on. Some are staying in the Church not because they accept the Church's more liberal direction, but because it is their Church. They grew up in the Church, they love this Church, they love our worship and prayer and pageantry and little gothic churches or huge contemporary spheres of worship. They find Elohim here, in this Church. Others find the same God in a different way, exactly because we're willing to stretch and change and become, exactly because we ordain women and the openly gay. Still others find el-Shaddai in the gentle comfort of people, of friends and neighbors, in the pews they've leased for years. Make no mistake, the Holy One is there—here—with them, and with us—but only in our love. We need our brothers and sisters, each with his and her gift offered as an oblation of life and labor and love, at the altar.

But we also need the charismatic, the conservative evangelical, the traditional anglo-catholic, and even the scriptural literalists—those with whom we do not see eye to eye, we need them, exactly because we *do not* see eye to eye; exactly because the charismatic discerns God's spirit in the free-flow of worship, in the gift of a tongue; and exactly because the scripture literalists draws lines the free-thinking progressive desperately needs, and divines the Divine between Levitical laws in a way I cannot understand. God is there, too, after all, flowing from those pages, rubbed raw from use, worn well by adoration.

And so it is, this quandary for Paul: *all things are lawful* at exactly the same time that *all things are decidedly not lawful.* It is not lawful to exercise a freedom that becomes divorce, that casts the right far from the left, segments, and creates disparate body parts, the right and the wrong, the Gnostic and the ordinary, the spiritual and the banal. The exact beauty of the Anglican tradition lies in our common worship, not in our common ideology or theology, and not even in our common morality. For we find God in that worship, in the bread broken, the wine poured, the body given, and the blood drunk. On knees, bent by love, at a holy rail, on holy spots.

Some of you will argue with me. Slavery, you will remind me, would still be an accepted institution if we followed your advice. Girls couldn't serve as acolytes. Gays will never be accepted, if we follow your advice. To which I would respond, this issue is not about slavery. This issue isn't even about the welcome of gays. It isn't about homosexuality. This issue is about the episcopacy, and who among us can become a bishop. But more deeply, this issue is about love. A love of God in us that is so wide, so expansive, that it believes all things and hopes all things and endures all things—a love that is patient and a love that trusts. Love trusts Jesus as Christ with His own Church—a huge love with bears' arms for bear hugs to embrace all people, not just those who look like I do.

Others of you will argue with me—there comes a time to call "sin" "sin," to take a stand, to stop the liberal and ungodly trajectory of the Church. But this is not about sin or the liberal trajectory of the Church. No, this matter is about love. A love of God in us that is so wide, so expansive, that it believes all things and hopes all things and endures all things—a love that is patient and a love that trusts. Love trusts Jesus as Christ with His own Church, a huge love with bears' arms for bear hugs to embrace all people, not just those who look like I do.

When I was a child, I thought like a child, I acted like a child. When I became an adult, I put away childish things (1 Cor. 13:11).

Paul was hopping mad at the Corinthians, and I'm betting he's hopping mad at us. They wouldn't set aside right and law and even their very notion of God and faith—for the person next to them. And yet, to lay down our life, our very life, in trust and holy expectation, is the call, the command. Lay down even what you believe deeply, for the anonymous saint sitting next to you. Paul sings in timeless harmony with Jesus, a duet, the call to love—the immutable call to love. It doesn't take Greek exegesis to understand the thirteenth chapter of First Corinthians, nor does it take Greek exegesis to understand when we don't do it well. Love.

In the end, Paul reminded the Corinthians that his letter is first and foremost about love: *Let all that you do be done in love* (1 Cor. 16:14). But we have forsaken love, and substituted righteousness, substituted self-righteousness, and God after all, God in Christ, is sad.

And so our sin, our collective, communal sin—sin with a capital "S"—is our failure to love.

chapter three
our father

Would You Have Followed Jesus?

The Jesus of Scripture was radical. He upended the status-quo, and made otherwise well-intentioned people uncomfortable. I would have been uncomfortable with Jesus, at least if I take Scripture seriously.

Jesus poked at the religious leaders, the Pharisees and Scribes; he irritated lawyers; he walked all over the good intentions of the DOT.com CEOs and Charles Schwab financial advisors—the establishment. These were well-meaning men trying precariously to balance the practice of Judaism in an increasingly complex society. Jesus walked all over *their* intentions.

Jesus was a rough-hewn prophet, someone most of

us would have shunned. Not the sweetsie-sappy-guy most of us re-imagine.

And that is why I am haunted by Wendell Barry's question: *"Would you have followed Jesus?"* Would you have said yes to this up-start preacher, this man who threatens your security, who emasculates your American way of life?

We're not talking comfort zone here. Love, yes. Comfort zone, no.

I might have been attracted to Jesus' miracles. I might have admired his clarity of truth, or the sense of anticipation building in the crowds that followed him. But would I have followed him? Would I have left my boat in the water, dropped my fishing net on the beach, and followed Jesus?

The disciples followed. They said, *"yes."* And it is to them, says John the Evangelist, that Jesus spoke at length simply on the night before he died. *"Abide in my love. As the Father has loved me, so have I loved you. Abide in my love."*

"Love one another as I have loved you."

"I am giving you these commands so that you may love one another."

Love one another. It isn't complicated. Abide in my love. Abide—as in abode, as in, *live there*, make love your home, sleep and eat there, keep house in love.

Jesus' love is not ethereal, esoteric, or removed from the scrambled-egg mess of daily life and actions. Jesus links love with commandment. *"If you love me, you will keep my commandment."* Jesus makes it sound as though you have a choice. You love by *doing: do the right thing to one another*—as though *doing* the right thing is love.

It isn't about doing. Doing the right thing is the result of love. It is love's by-product.

What Jesus means is this: those of you who treat life as a commandment to be lived, a checklist of *do's* and *don't's*, a jigsaw puzzle of right and wrong—I set you free from all of that, and bind you simply to love, for if you *abide in*, live in, exist and be nourished by love, then you *will do the rest.*

You *will* be good to others if you make love your home. You *will* treat others as yourself. You won't steal or covet or commit adultery if you sleep in love's condominium.

Jesus proffered a new commandment: love one another. Abide in love.

Two elements attend love in Christ: *love from God,* you have to believe God loves you, really and honestly loves you, despite your junk, despite the overlay of your false self. You are loved, you are accepted, you are God's own child, loved completely, with no greater love.

And *love of the other.* Love is an action verb with *other,* real people, as its direct object. For you to love one another, there must be an *other.* You can't live both as a hermit and in love. Community is required. And guess what? Love of others sets you free, free as a bird from the tyranny of self.

George MacDonald wrote, *"The love of our neighbor is the only door out of the dungeon of self, where we mope and mow, striking sparks, and rubbing phosphorescences out of the walls, and blowing our own breath in our own nostrils, instead of issuing to the fair sunlight of God, the sweet winds of the universe."*[10]

Blowing our own breath in our own nostrils. I need *your breath* in my nostrils to live. I need mouth to mouth resuscitation from you, your love, your care, your undying loyalty. My salvation is found in your breath, a gift from you.

Abide in my love. In community. Make that your home.

My wonderful little church on the side of a Sausalito hillside—Christ Church—holds a prayer vigil overnight Maundy Thursday to Good Friday. The sacristy becomes a chapel, with a prie-dieu in front of a makeshift altar, a veiled cross, and votive candles like stars at night light the room.

Two years ago, I signed up for the 5:00–6:00 a.m. shift. From the time the Maundy Thursday service ended in the dramatic and moving stripping of the altar to the time of the crucifixion good people kept watch, and waited and prayed in that temporary chapel.

I arrived at exactly 5:00 a.m. My friend, Liz O'Keefe, preceded me. I tapped on the door lightly as I entered the chapel, turning the doorknob slowly so as not to startle Liz. Maybe she'd fallen asleep, I had imagined.

But Liz hadn't fallen asleep. She sat in her chair, silently, reverently, as if waiting for...

I joined Liz, and together we sat—we just sat. After about five minutes, Liz stood up and walked out. Her time was finished. And I realized as she walked out, and as I sat there alone in that space, the space wasn't just a room in which prayers had been offered, it was a room in which prayer lived. Prayer lived in that little chapel. It hung in the air, it swirled about me as I sat there. I breathed prayer as air.

I tried not to disturb the prayer hanging there, so I sat, absorbed by the prayer.

Love is like that. "*Abide in my love,*" Jesus said simply. Live there, make that your home. Walk into love as into a prayer room, and do nothing to dispel the love already hanging in the air. The love you breathe as air.

It is, of course, a radical love, a love that considers the other first, before yourself, that gives and gives and then gives some more.

When called for, it is a hard love, as in upending tables at Temple and rebuking religious leaders. And a soft love when appropriate, as in welcoming the prodigal home. It is a love that wrestles and tussles from time to time, as the church struggles to find its way, but it is also a love that secures, seals you as Christ's own forever among people who, with you, choose that love above all else.

Live in *that love*. Make your home in *that love*.

Would I have followed Jesus had I lived 2000

years ago? Yes, I believe I would have, but not because I would have chosen to follow, as though I would have had a choice. Rather, love would have compelled me to follow. The love that surrounded this man as air would have pulled me against my very nature, outside of myself, and into this brave new world of community.

Matthew and the Lord's Prayer

Jesus offered the Lord's Prayer as community prayer. A prayer for people in love with one another, for a people abiding in love. I have always heard teachers treat the Lord's Prayer as a template for individual prayer, but it isn't. The Lord's Prayer is foremost a church prayer, for and about the new community, a prayer about God's kingdom and thus God's community. It is thus our prayer, and it is answered as we pray it together. Applying a common faith, the faith of Christ.

Matthew introduces the Lord's Prayer at the Sermon on the Mount. Jesus is the new Moses, issuing a *new* way of looking at the law, teaching the *heart,* the meaning, the intent and philosophy of the law. Both Matthew and Jesus are faithful to God's promise made over and over again to Israel. No New Testament (Covenant) for Matthew and Jesus; this is a natural continuation of the original. The Church, this emerging community of Jew and Gentile, however, has supplanted the nation of Israel as the inheritor of the promise.

Thus, Matthew is both quite Jewish and quite anti-establishment (especially religious establishment). The Jewish leaders are the reprobate, reprehensible inheritors of the authoritarian religious structure of the Hebrew people. Never mind that their intentions might have been acceptable to you and to me—that they were caught in a political and godly maelstrom between the Roman authorities and God. The Roman authorities demanded loyalty to Caesar. God demanded loyalty only to God. (Hence their question about whether to pay the tax—they felt trapped between God and Caesar, and expected Jesus to feel the same thing. He didn't, nor should we!)

The Jewish leaders are trying so hard to pacify God by observing the Law that they have forgotten the meaning, the heart, of the Law. Matthew shows Jesus expending considerable effort deconstructing the authority of the religious leaders and constructing the authority of the Church, deconstructing a false understanding of the Law and reconstructing the heart of the Law.

Matthew and Deconstruction. First, the deconstruction. Tension builds between Jesus and the religious authorities throughout Matthew, but it isn't until Holy Week that Jesus declares final the divorce between God and the nominal nation of Israel.[11] An important note should be offered. Although Jesus declares divorce between God and Israel, he focuses primarily on those religious leaders who have led the people astray. Jesus constantly woos the people of

Israel back to God, such as at the Sermon on the Mount. But clearly, the Church as structure is now supplanting Israel as structure, if only because of the religious leaders.

Jesus enters Jerusalem on Palm Sunday to great fanfare (Matt. 21:1), and the whole city is in turmoil. He heads straight to the Temple and throws out the money-changers, men and women who would make a buck at God's expense (Matt. 21:12-13). The Temple is God's house, for worship, for adoration, not for personal gain.

Jesus returns to the Temple the next day, but only after cursing a barren fig tree on his way (Matt. 21:18, 19). The fig tree in the Hebrew Scriptures represents Israel. Israel is fruitless. God never intended Israel to keep the promise to itself, but planned for Israel to become a blessing to the entire earth (see, e.g., Isaiah 66:18; *compare* Matt. 28:18-20, the work of the new community). There is no fruit, there is no gift, and both Israel and the cursed tree wither.

When Jesus enters the Temple that second day to teach, the religious leaders challenge him. He proves to be their debating superior, and embarrasses them severely. Their authority is baseless.[12] Nominal authority is not the same as *real* authority. Jesus shows theirs to be nominal, devoid of God's blessing, and thereby rejected.

Jesus tells the parable of the two sons (Matt. 22:28-32), the one who said he'd work and didn't, and the one who said he wouldn't, and did. Israel is the son who promised to work, but didn't. Who did the will of the Father? Certainly not that son.

Jesus continues with the transparent parable of the landowner who planted a vineyard (Matt. 22:33-46). The man leases (entrusts) the vineyard to wicked tenants who seize, thrash and kill servants sent by the landowner to collect rent. The leaders are the wicked tenants; this time, the vineyard is God's people. The religious leaders become so instantly incensed as they listen to the parable, that they decide to arrest Jesus, which, of course, is the ironic response anticipated by the parable—the seizing and killing of the Son to continue an illegal occupation of the vineyard.

The parable of the wedding feast drives home the point that those who think they are in are out (Matt. 22:1-14). The invited guests don't come, so the wild celebration is thrown open to anyone who will come, those in the highway or byway, in the field or town. The unexpected and not a select party-list are welcome. Not Israel, and certainly not the leaders.[13]

At the end of this litany of parables and confrontations, Jesus concludes with the point of it all, the bulls-eye of love. The Greatest Commandment, *Love the Lord your God, with all that you are and all that you have* (Matt. 22:34-40). And the second that is so much like it that perhaps you cannot accomplish one without accomplishing the other, *Love your neighbor as yourself*. The law and the prophets are not abrogated after all, but fulfilled here, in these two laws.[14]

Matthew and Reconstruction. And so, Jesus does not

abrogate, but deconstructs the old way, the promise made to Abraham, Moses, the Hebrew children, and the prophets. He deconstructs in order to rebuild, to clarify, and to give a deeper meaning to the covenant. The religious leaders are intransigent bullies attempting to manipulate and control truth, who treat truth as a commodity for sale. Metaphorically, they man tables of trade in God's Temple.

Simultaneous with deconstruction, Matthew's Jesus constructs a new group, a new Israel, a new people, the church.[15] Construction is Matthew's *real* purpose in writing, and a main purpose to Jesus' life and ministry (see Matt. 26:61). Jesus is building the new community like Moses built the former community.

Hence, Jesus is Moses redux, or better yet, new and improved, a *messianic* Moses, forming a new *messianic* community as heir to Abraham.[16]

So it is, that this *messianic* Moses gathers people around him early in his ministry, not to abrogate the Law and the Prophets, but to fulfill them (Matt. 5:17). Honoring the Law requires *more*, not less, effort on your part. *Not only do you refrain from killing, don't even be angry with your brother; not only do you not commit adultery, don't even look with lust at another woman.* Worse, the justice to which you imagine yourself entitled creates the wrong attitude, so seek not justice, but rather, offer passive nonresistance. *Not an eye for an eye, but rather, to the one who slaps your right cheek, offer the left as well. If anyone orders you to go one mile, go two. Give to the one who asks, and if someone wants to borrow, do not turn him away* (Matt. 5:20-48).

Next Jesus teaches this fledgling *messianic community*, this new inheritor of the Promise, what devotion to God entails. Devotion is paying attention to God when you do your good works, not to others. Don't seek to be noticed (Matt. 6:1-4). Give alms secretly, *do not let your left hand know what your right is doing.* Do not pray so others will compliment or praise you for it; pray so God will hear you (Matt. 6:5-6).

The Lord's Prayer in the Sermon on the Mount is the heart of Jesus' teaching on prayer, a worship template for the new community. Not for the individual, this prayer is to be prayed by, prayed for, and owned within the *messianic community*. Quite startling to our individualistic society—so startling, in-fact, that we subliminally ignore it—is this: the Lord's Prayer contains no singular pronouns. No "I," no "my," but only "Our," only "us," only "we."

> ***Our*** Father,
> who art in heaven,
> thy *kingdom come*,
> [which means] *thy will be done*,
> on earth as it is in heaven.
> [what kingdom on earth will look like:]
> [no hunger:]Give ***us*** this day ***our*** daily bread,
> [forgiveness and reconciliation:]
> forgive ***us*** our trespasses,
> as ***we*** forgive those who trespass against ***us***.

[the subjection of evil,
beginning in the community:]
Lead **us** not into temptation,
but deliver **us** from evil.
For Thine is the *kingdom*,
[which means:] the power,
and the glory, forever. Amen.

Again, this prayer contains only plural pronouns, and no first person pronoun whatsoever. Even when you pray the prayer privately, you are joining as two or more gathered in His name, as community. Jesus established this prayer as if to emphasize *unity* as kingdom.

Almost as startling is this: this prayer is solely about kingdom, about building God's kingdom on earth in and through the community. God's rule, God's domain, God's territory—let it be here as it is in heaven, let it be here *that* way. In fact, let your kingdom color the earth like food coloring colors water, permeates it, forever changes it. The *messianic community* is to spread as food coloring throughout the world—a precept emphasized by the Great Commission at the conclusion to Matthew: make disciples of all nations, baptizing them in the name of the Father and of the Son and of the Holy Spirit (Matt. 28:18-20). The Holy Spirit = food coloring.

And what are the marks of the community that prays for God's kingdom to come to earth? One, there is no need, for daily bread, sustenance, is common. The economy of God's kingdom is different from the economy of this world. The economy of this world is based upon the old economic precept of *allocation of scarce resources*. Prices determined by supply and demand. God's economy is based upon generous supply created when God's people give away from themselves to one another. Kingdom, where need defines supply.

Two, in God's kingdom, forgiveness and not the demand for justice pervades. It is a world in which you walk two miles when asked to walk one, in which you loan to anyone wanting to borrow. You could demand justice, but you offer forgiveness instead. Why? Because, at last, you recognize in yourself the same need, forgiveness. You recognize in yourself the same tenuous thread that ties you to the Divine, Rahab's scarlet cord of grace.

Three, in God's kingdom, temptation is not God's design, but rather the work of evil. God does not tempt us, but protects us from evil.

The Sermon on the Mount continues, of-course, with more improvisations on the Law and the Prophets, but at its heart is this little prayer, the *Our Father*, a *messianic community* prayer.

The Lord's Prayer: A Prayer of Unity

And so it is: you cannot pray *Our Father* with integrity and hate your brother, or even your enemy. Using "our" with Father is your instant acknowledgement that you are not an only child, that you don't own God, that you can't know everything that is to be known about God. You cannot pray *Our Father* and demand your own way to the exclusion of others. You just cannot do it.

In the context of the Episcopal Church, *Our* means that you, who hold vastly different positions on the ordination of Gene Robinson as Bishop from mine, acknowledge the possible fallibility of your position. I, too, acknowledge the possible fallibility of my position. I don't own God. There is always an "our" with whom I must contend.

Our also means you cannot hate the person with whom you pray. Last year, when I preached on the Lord's Prayer, I told my San Francisco Bay area congregation that one cannot say "Our" Father and hate George Bush (an avowed Christian). People in the Bay area hate George Bush viscerally. But, you can't say "Our" Father with integrity and hate George Bush.

Had I been preaching the same sermon in my home state of Tennessee, I would have said, *you can't say Our Father and hate Hilary Clinton.* People in the American South harbor the same visceral hate against Hilary Clinton that people in the Bay area harbor against George Bush. That type of visceral hate is antithetical to the Lord's Prayer, to its first two words. You can't pray "our", hate your brother whom you can see, and claim to love God who you cannot see.

Also, forgiveness—not just forgiveness sought by another, but the forgiveness the other doesn't even realize she needs—that forgiveness must be offered in order to say the Lord's Prayer with integrity.

In short, the Lord's Prayer is both *the* prayer of Christ, and a template. It is our formal agreement to do our best, with God's help, to live Jesus' teaching offered on the Mount. You accept *that* Law and Prophets. You accede to *that* Law and Prophets. You choose to be in *that* community, and you yield your own design of all else—even your conception of morality and human psychology—to the person in the pew next to you. *Our* Father.

In that kingdom, in that community, those who are strong yield to those who are weak. Or better, yet, both strong and weak yield to one another.

Unfortunately, we Episcopalians and Anglicans *are not living into our prayer, are not acting like Jesus the messianic Moses instructed.* We are not abiding in love. We are not acceding to *the more excellent way.*

Perhaps, the Episcopal majority approving Gene Robinson should have yielded to the Episcopal minority. Perhaps the Episcopal minority should have trusted God and Jesus as head of the Church. Perhaps all of us should have trusted the Christ in one another. In the end, our living salvation is not found in the correctness of our position, but in the humility we engage along the way, the submission we offer, the love we offer.

After all, isn't what we do most often less important than why and how we do it? Purity of motive and method are important to Jesus. What else could

Jesus have meant when he told givers to give in secret, prayers to pray in closets? Isn't the widow with the mite the greatest giver? Motive counts. Love counts.

Do we love? Abide in my love, Jesus advised the disciples gathered around that long table, with wine and bread as staples for ritual. The ritual itself contemplates love, contemplates unity, contemplates a whole and complete, and not divided, *messianic community*.

I don't have the exact answer on where we should go from here. I'm writing simply because we don't look like the Church Scripture defines or Jesus established. Rather, we look and sound quite a bit like the religious leaders in need of deconstruction. Cause and not Christ has become central, and there is no health in us.

Community Devotion

If I were to point a way forward, it would be the way of devotion. I met a fellow at a party not long ago. This man was on his third marriage. When our host told him that I am the local Episcopal clergy, he immediately started talking about his marriage. *I would like to talk to couples about to get married—your couples. Can I help you?*

I was taken aback. Nobody's ever made that offer to me. *Oh,* I said. *How many times have you been married?*

Three.

How long this last time? I asked.

One and a half years.

Hmmm. What would you tell people?

Easy, he said. At this point, I started looking for a way to escape the conversation. Marriage is anything but easy; it is hard work, indeed. But he continued.

Easy. In my other marriages, I was consumed by my own needs. By what I needed from my wife. This time, I decided to be devoted. Wholly devoted. To be consumed by my wife's needs. I do that, I pay attention to that.

Devoted. I laughed to myself when he said this— because, well, he was right. Devotion to another. We mistakenly imagine our devotion to God in Christ to be sufficient. It isn't. Devotion to one another is the key to a successful Christian Church. Devotion, the giving of self to another. Our Father. Not My Father.

Abide in my love. Live there, make your bed there, in *that* house. I am compelled outside of myself to follow *that* love.

chapter four
the gifts of god
for the people of god

Mary Ransom was the Christian educator in my first parish, St. Luke's, in Cleveland, Tennessee. She was 83 years old at the time, her face was lined from years in the sun, and the children adored her. They adored her because Mary adored them—genuine love.

Mary understood that you teach children by example. Children learn mostly by absorption—from who we are and our actions, not from our words. Words are secondary and serve to interpret actions and life experiences, but what we do, our deeds, are the primary instructors. Children *become* the people around them. That is exactly why Mary used to say with a twinkle in her eye, *Your actions speak so loud, I can't hear what you say.*

The Action of Worship

The Holy Eucharist is worship in action. It is, as our *Book of Common Prayer* says, the principal *act* of Christian worship on the Lord's Day (BCP 13). Intentioned physical actions can be prayer—crossing oneself, kneeling, bowing the head, laying a hand on the telephone,[17] even jogging.[18] The celebration of the Eucharist is an *act* of worship.[19] The words matter, but only secondarily.

The Body of Christ assembles itself in church-form, members coming from short distances, from long distances. The diverse members of the Body of Christ gathering together, bringing to the table the product of our hands, the *offerings and oblations of our life and labor*.[20] Life and labor take the form of bread and wine, and in the ultimate *act* of unity, the priest, as representative of the community, physically blesses the product of our hands, consecrates it to become the gift of God to the same community in return, the lifeblood of eternity, the body and blood of Christ. This mystical union of the temporal with the eternal, transcending time and space, uniting disparate members into *one*, is the ultimate *act* of worship.

No individual accomplishes this miracle. No priest, no bishop, no specially appointed person accomplishes this miracle. The *act* of miracle is accomplished by the community, by the presence and *unity* of the community—hence the word, *community,* as the community remembers, recalls, reenacts, re-stages, the Christ event, just like the old childrens' educational series that taught history through television, *You are there*. You are there, in the Eucharist, at the table with the twelve on the night before our Lord died, when Jesus once again takes the bread, blesses it, breaks it, and distributes it. He takes the cup, and blesses it, and passes it. You are there, and it is your *act* of worship in comm-*union* with this Christ, together in comm-*union* with God, in comm-*union* with the twelve, in comm-*union* with the witnesses of ages. In comm-*union* with one another.

The work of the people, my seminary professor Marion Hatchett called it. Liturgy is the work of the people, all of us acting together in the ultimate donation of self to the whole: unity.

The Action of Service

Scripture commends this act of unity to the Church. You find the institution of the Eucharist in all three Synoptic (*seeing together*) Gospels (Matt. 26:26-29; Lk. 22:19-20; Mk. 14:22-25; *cf. Jn. 13*). The evangelist John *interprets* the act of the Eucharist through the washing of the feet. After Supper, instead of offering the cup, Jesus rises from the table, strips naked in the ultimate *act* of vulnerability, puts a towel around his waist as a servant, and washes the disciples' feet—even Judas' feet—and then tells the impetuous and protesting Peter, *if you do not let me wash your feet, you can have no part of me* (Jn. 13:8). Peter retorts, *well then, wash all of me*. And Jesus does.

John is, of course, telling us that the ultimate *act* of

worship—in which God in Christ involves us, welcomes us, and communes with us—is not private,
but includes the whole of the Body of Christ—the
Peter's and the Judas', the good and the bad—and
becomes worship only when *love* is involved. Jesus in
John continues after the washing by saying exactly
that—*I give you a new commandment: love one another;
just as I have loved you, you also must love one another.
By this love you have for one another, everyone will know
that you are my disciples* (Jn. 13:33, Jerusalem Bible).

Also, *Remain in my love.... This is my commandment:
love one another, as I have loved you* (Jn. 15:16).[21]

The Action of Unity

Just a short while later, still at table (think
Eucharist), Jesus offers the great *priestly* prayer, and
prays for the disciples, and by extension, us: *that they
may be one, just as the Father and the Son are one* (Jn.
17:12). And again, *May they all be one. Father, may
they be one in us, as you are in me and I am in you...com-
pletely one* (Jn. 17:21, 23, Jerusalem Bible). The
meaning seems obvious; make them so much a part
of one another, and then, as a body, so much a part
of us, you and me.

Which is decidedly *not* where the Episcopal
Church and Anglican Communion are today. Nor are
the esteemed bishops and primates, who would do
well to remember that the only people—besides
money-changers—with whom Jesus became visceral-

ly angry were the religious leaders. (As a priest, I remind myself of this fact regularly.)

Like Jesus at the Last Supper, Paul also interprets the Eucharist to be a worship *act* characterized by unity (1 Cor. 11:17-34). Instantly he chides the Corinthian Church for their divisions—and especially for their selfishness. *In the first place, I hear that when you all come together as a community, there are separate factions among you, and I half believe it* (1 Cor. 11:18). Paul flatly states that it is not, in fact, *the Lord's Supper that you are eating* (11:20).

It is disunity against which Paul speaks baldly, when he directs the Corinthians to *recollect* themselves before eating. When you fail to recollect, he tells them, you are eating and drinking in an unworthy fashion, eating and drinking without *recognizing the Body [of Christ],* and eating and drinking your own condemnation. Bishop Akinola's fear of eating the Eucharist with sinners does not make sense in light of Paul's overarching concern for the unity of the Body throughout. Paul is not railing against notorious sin in the way Bishop Akinola imagines; he is railing against disunity. It is the disunity of the Corinthian church, caused especially by those with "knowledge," that is the appropriating sin resulting in condemnation (see generally, 1 Cor. 11:23-34, Jerusalem Bible). Eating and drinking duplicitously, as though unified, when actually quite divided, is the *eating and drinking without recognizing the Body*. Does this sound familiar? By feigning to avoid of sin,

Bishop Akinola actually engaged in sin. Of the worst kind.

The Words We Pray

Moreover, it is for unity that we pray when re-en-*acting* the Eucharist. The general confession is a community confession, a confession of the Unit, and not of multiple individuals who happen to be collected together in the same room. We confess as a Unit exactly because the Unit, and not just individuals, will receive the disparate pieces of the Body and Blood—to reconstruct Christ in us, to create one Unit from the many. (All of this prayer action occurs not for ourselves, but for the world—Christ and the Church, broken for the world. The Eucharist is the first step in a movement of God's grace to the world.)

Perhaps this is why we pray for unity so succinctly in the Eucharistic Prayers:

Rite I, Prayer I: *[We pray] that we, and all others who shall be partakers of this Holy Communion, may worthily receive the most precious Body and Blood of thy Son Jesus Christ, be filled with thy grace and heavenly benediction, and made one body with him, that he may dwell in us, and we in him* (BCP 336; see also Rite I, Prayer II, BCP 342).

Rite II, Prayer A: *Sanctify us also that we may faithfully receive this holy Sacrament, and serve you in* **unity**, *constancy and peace* (BCP 369).

Prayer B: **Unite** *us to your Son in his sacrifice, that* **we** *may be acceptable through him...*(as opposed to Unite us...that *each of us may be acceptable...*) (BCP 369).

Prayer C: *Let the grace of this Holy Communion make us one body, one spirit in Christ, that we may worthily serve the world in his name* (BCP 372).

Prayer D: *Grant that all who share this bread and cup may become one body and one spirit, a living Sacrifice in Christ, to the praise of your Name.... Remember, Lord, your one holy catholic and apostolic Church, redeemed by the blood of your Christ. Reveal its unity, guard its faith, and preserve it in peace* (BCP 375).[22]

Prayer D is ancient, dating to the earliest church, a time when the Church emphasized its unity. The *Didache*, or *Training*, the earliest documented training manual for Christians, offers this simple prayer: *Remember, Lord, your church, to save [her] from every evil and to perfect [her] in your love and to gather [her] together from the four winds [as] the sanctified into your kingdom which you have prepared for her, because yours is the power and the glory forever* (10:5).

The *Training* also calls for unity in moral conduct: *You will not cause dissention: (1) you will reconcile those fighting; (2) you will judge justly; (3) you will not take [into account] social status [when it comes time] to reprove against failings* (4:3).

Like Paul, the *Training* ties the Eucharist to reconciliation and unity: *Everyone, on the other hand, having a conflict with a companion, do not let [him/her] come together with you until they have been reconciled, in order that your sacrifice may not be defiled* (14:2).

Even these quite early Christians interpret unity

and reconciliation as a part of the *act* of Christian worship. Failure to reconcile is the capstone sin of the Body of Christ; intransigence blocks the mysterious rejoining of the disparate pieces of the Loaf into One Body, One Christ.

Like the *Training*, Jesus commands (as opposed to recommends) reconciliation before worship: *[when you] remember that your brother [or sister] has something against you, leave your offering there before the altar,*[23] *go and be reconciled with your brother [or sister] first, and then come back and present your offering* (Matt. 5:23). This Scripture is absolutely unambiguous. If we were to take it seriously, either there would be no Eucharist, or perhaps, we might learn to get along. Not agree, get along.

The Actions We Accomplish

The Christian act of worship in the Eucharist is the ultimate act of Christian unity. It is sin to re-enact the Eucharist as a church divided, at least to the extent you have control over reconciliation.[24] Like I said before: it is mortal sin, as in the death of the Church.

Which is why it was so surprising several years ago when Bishop Akinola, the primate of the Church of Nigeria, refused to worship with his counterpart, Bishop Frank Griswold, the former Presiding Bishop of the Episcopal Church. Bishop Akinola insisted that Bishop Rowan Williams, Archbishop of Canterbury, offer him the Eucharist in a separate room. What is more surprising is that Bishop

Williams acceded to his request. Bishop Williams should have insisted upon reconciliation (not agreement) before serving either communion.

History repeated itself earlier this year (2007) in Tanzania, the week before Ash Wednesday, when twelve (or so) primates refused to take communion with the new Presiding Bishop of the Episcopal Church, Bishop Katherine Jefforts-Schori. Refusing communion as comm-*union*, they claimed, was to remind us of the brokenness of our communion. They are correct in that the comm-*union* is broken, but the moral imperative is not to go off by oneself to take communion, but to reconcile. Leave the altar, not set up a different one. To fail to do so is to consume the body and blood in an unworthy fashion.

No washing of feet, here. No service above all, no naked vulnerability, no yielding one's own interpretation of Scripture to that of another, and in short, no love. No love at all, at the ultimate love feast, the Eucharist. No unity at all, at the ultimate symbol and sacrament of peace. I can't help but wonder whether separate communion might just be the abomination of desolation set up in the Holy Place. Let the reader beware (Matt. 28:15).

This is sin—community sin, the failure to reconcile.

Frederick Beuchner brings the concept of sin into the twenty-first century. *The power of sin is centrifugal. When at work in a human life, it tends to push everything out toward the periphery. Bits and pieces go flying off until only the core is left. Eventually bits and pieces of the core itself go flying off until in the end nothing at all is left. 'The wages of sin is death' is Saint Paul's way of saying the same thing.*[25]

Sin, Beuchner continues, is the very thing that pushes you away from God, the world, society, nature. It widens the gap, he says, even the gaps within yourself.

To be sure, unity for unity's sake—without addressing the moral issues of our day—would constitute sin. But dividing Christ the way we Episcopalians and Anglicans have is patently unacceptable. To let that divide, to let that conquer, is itself a yielding to sin, is itself sin.

Anglicanism gets it right, so oddly, because it rallies around worship—not around theologies (believer's baptism like the Baptists), or around confessions (like the Lutherans' Augsburg Confession). I say *oddly*, meaning that the foundation of Anglicanism is suspect, driven in part by politics (Henry VIII, Edward VI, Mary, and Elizabeth), and a politics to separate, to reform, and to compromise. But the compromise, the *via media*, the middle way, means that we don't rally around doctrinal agreement, but worship. We call it the *Book of Common Prayer*, and our central theological and moral activity is action, the Eucharist. We are not dogmatic, we are action-oriented. Action in Worship, and Worship in service.

To be sure, we recite the Nicene Creed, but we wonder about its meaning. We study a catechism that adds loose flesh to bones, but we don't pretend it stakes claims on complex theological issues. Indeed, statements like, *God still speaks to us through the Bible* (BCP 853), hardly answer the question of the role of Scripture in daily life.

The Thirty-Nine Articles, treated as *historic* in our Book of Common Prayer, are both arcane and disputed. Almost nobody agrees with all of the articles (does anybody really think that just *some* are chosen from before time to salvation? Article XVII, BCP 871).

Some would argue that Holy Scriptures form the *only* basis for theology—and I wish that this were true. But Scriptures by their very nature cannot accomplish this task, as Scriptures are—when all is said and done—just what our Catechesis says they are: ...*books written by the people of the New/Old Covenant[s], under the inspiration of the Holy Spirit, to [1] show God at work in nature and history[, and (2)] to set forth the life and teachings of Jesus and to proclaim the Good News of the Kingdom for all people* (BCP 853). There will not be (nor *can* there be) any agreement on Scriptural interpretation. Moreover, Anglicanism has always relied upon Tradition and Reason in trinity with Scripture, not on Scripture alone.

In fact, there are no two people who agree fully on the interpretation of Scripture. I once met a man who tried his level best to observe each *jot and tittle* of the Law, including the moral, dietary, and worship codes of the Torah. He was the only Christian I know who ever came close to following Scriptural dictates—but he wasn't Anglican or Episcopalian, and I have never found one single Anglican or Episcopalian who bothered to try. It is time to stop using Scripture to support prejudice and preference.

We wonder why our churches aren't growing, why so many are faltering. As Mary Ransom might say, *what we do speaks so loud, the world can't hear what we say.* People are avoiding us in droves. Who wants to attend a bickering, divided church? People are seeking truth, truth as spirit and depth and meaning, but all they can find behind our doors is division.

We have become the dysfunctional family that is more at home with the fight than with functionality. Our fight is the action that speaks loudly, when it should be the action of the Eucharist speaking. The unity of the *holy* Eucharist. The cosmic and thrilling act that brings the kingdom of heaven to earth and earth to heaven, that transports truth through the soul as oxygen through blood, a blood pulse. The complete act of Love, of intercourse, of God becoming us, and us becoming God. Maybe that is what Jesus meant when he said, *they will know you are Christians by your love for one another* (John 13:35). Or more darkly later, when he said through John, *I have this against you; you have lost your first love* (Rev. 2:4).

Ahh, there it is, the passion, the absolute whirling dervish of complete abandon, where love thrives. You have lost that love, Anglicans, Episcopalians. But you have not lost hope. Love can be recovered by returning—to primal action, to worship.

chapter five
welcoming the light

The Darkness

There is such a thing as Original Sin, only it isn't what you think. Original Sin is the pall of darkness covering our world.

We live in a room shrink-wrapped by time and space, enshrouded and governed by darkness (see Jn. 1:5). We breathe evil as oxygen in this dark place. It isn't a choice. We are born into it. Division, hate, bitterness, war, sectarianism, racism, sexism, fear, doubt, even pessimism. Humanity cannot escape the evil. There is no health in us.

Indeed, there is beauty and wonder and love here, joy and family and closeness. But this Eden-earth is canopied as a rainforest. We see the beauty of Eden darkly.

God unbounded by time and space, God as ubiquitous, God living simultaneously in all places and at all times: that God as infinite light entered into the room of this world through the doorway of a virgin. God as the absolute of good and love and light voluntarily subjected herself (or himself, if you prefer[26]) to, in Scripture's words, the shroud of darkness, the *prince of this world*,[27] the darkness personified.

God by incarnation submitted to the devil, breathed deeply the devil's oxygen, was tempted in the wilderness to become one with the devil, and was, at the end of it all, murdered by the devil. Death strangled life; evil trumped love and entombed God.

The Christian message is stark, compelling, and horrifying. Absolute, perfect, and infinite good and love and light submitted by passive non-resistance to absolute, perfect, and finite evil and hate and darkness. To death. Good Friday became the devil's holy day.

The Light

But Good Friday is not the endgame. Easter is. The expression of nuclear power as at Hiroshima and Nagasaki to end WWII is *exactly* God's plan, only darkness and not people is the target. It isn't just that Jesus rises from the dead on Easter morning, death itself replaces Jesus in the tomb. As Paul writes, death is the ultimate enemy to suffer defeat (1 Cor. 15:26).

The power of the Christian promise is not that God is compassionate, nor that God is our companion when life gets tough—no matter how accurate both truisms might be. The power of Christianity is this: the darkness has been rendered a mere illusionist, acting by slight of hand. Fear is the only power darkness has left. Life and light and eternity bested darkness long ago; we are victors already. Life is ours now. Life through death. Easter through Good Friday.

And therein lies the horror: we live because we first die. *I have been crucified with Christ,* Paul writes, *and it is no longer I who live, but Christ lives in me. And the life which I now live in the flesh, I live by faith...* (para. Gal. 2:20). Jesus, too, understands that we gain life only through death: *take up your cross and follow me* (see, e.g., Lk. 9:23, 24). *In union with Christ we have imitated his death, we shall also imitate him in his resurrection* (Rom. 6:5).

The ancient rite of Baptism incorporates this theology of symbiosis:

We thank you, Almighty God, for the gift of water.. . . of Baptism. In it we are buried with Christ in his death. By it we share in his resurrection. Through it we are reborn by the Holy Spirit (BCP 306).

Baptism is not some arcane rite by which otherwise innocent babies cursed with actual sin are cleansed and, as my seminary professor liked to quip, *slapped into the Kingdom,* saved from hell in the nick-o-time. Baptism isn't a fire insurance policy, nor is baptism primarily about forgiveness.

Baptism is about darkness and light, death and life. It is about Original Sin, and its defeat as a power in our lives. But it is also about submitting first to death. We identify fully with and accede to the power of death at the cross *exactly because* we trust in God as Son submitting completely on the cross: *Into your hands I commend my spirit.* We give up the ghost, the sky turns dark.

Which may be why the priest marks the baptismal candidate on the forehead with the sign of the cross, *Christ's own forever.* The cross is the mark of your death. You are no longer your own, you are *Christ's own forever*—a dead man walking.

Following Jesus always leads to the cross, for God and good and others in the defeat of evil. *He who will save his life will lose it; he who will lose his life for my sake will find it* (Lk. 9:24). *Every stitch* of Christian ethic originates at the foot of self-sacrifice. Not self-preservation.

But the cross at baptism becomes the mark of life. My life, the one that is hidden with God in Christ. (Col. 3:3) I am alive because I have died!

Note the severe poignancy of Ash Wednesday. The priest marks the forehead with the same cross and oil as at baptism, marking the penitent simultaneously with death and life: *You are dust, and to dust you shall return,* and the unspoken reminder, you are *Christ's own forever.* Again, death is life's womb.

Original Sin. Original Sin isn't some stain on the soul inherited from parents. Original Sin isn't about what one has done or left undone. Original Sin is about the state of affairs—the condition of the world, the air we breathe. The air is polluted, and the condition of the world is dark. That Original Sin is sin with a capital "S," and is about us—all of us, and not any one of us. Original Sin is collective darkness, the hardness of the heart of a humanity that long ago rejected its God. It doesn't matter whether you believe in Eden literally or metaphorically, the result is the same. Humanity preferred, and most often still prefers, evil over good, the devil over God. War over peace. Death over life.

God as Son breathed evil as oxygen when born into this world, and so do we. From the minute we are born, we become polluted with the oxygen of evil that we breathe. We become estranged from love, estranged from life, estranged from good, estranged from God, and estranged from others. Our estrangement is also Original Sin, the state of affairs requiring the saving act of Christ. We need to be saved from the evil of isolation.

Baptism saves us (1 Pet. 3:21). Born again into Christ, into community, we are fitted and joined with others, into a living organism of love and acceptance. *What God has joined together, let no one put asunder.*

Love. Paul doesn't write about the power of self-sacrificial love for the poetry of the words, but for a power-filled reason. The power of life is found in a love that does not *insist on its own way; ...that bears all things, believes all things, hopes all things, endures all things* (1 Cor. 13:4-7). Love submits to the Other, as Jesus at the Cross.

This love is the ultimate, and perhaps only,

Scriptural imperative: *[L]ove the Lord your God with all your heart, with all your soul, and with all your mind.... [L]ove your neighbor as yourself* (Jer. Bible, Mt. 22:37). All of the law and the prophets hang, depend upon, and are interpreted by a love that becomes at least equal to, if not greater than, love of self.

The exotic beauty of love is rather simple. Love as light dispels darkness. Love is a positive force that overcomes. Love casts out fear. Love keeps Original Sin at bay.

The issue facing us, then, is this: what happens when we stop loving, when we stop being a community of love? *What good is salt that has lost its saltiness?* (Matt. 5:13). It is fit only to be trampled underfoot.

Rather than self-sacrifice forming our ethic, rather than love binding us, we in both the Episcopal Church and the broader Anglican Communion have formed ethic by argument, by besting one another, by being *right* rather than by loving.

It doesn't matter whether the position one holds on the issue of Gene Robinson's ordination and on homosexuality is technically and morally correct. It really does not matter. The reason it doesn't matter is because we are asked by God to trust in Jesus as the Christ to be and act as the head of the Body, the head of the Church. We trust Jesus to take care of things, to bring things around to a right theology, and we trust Jesus because we are deeply aware of our own fallibility, our own humanity, that we've been wrong before, we'll be wrong again, and in all likelihood, each of us is wrong now—at least in part. In fact, I guarantee it.

Even if, perchance, there is one of us who is not wrong technically on the issue, he or she is still wrong. As my parents used to tell me, you can be right as rain and still wrong. Remember, Jesus pointed to the sinner beating his chest for mercy as the one who received mercy, not the righteous Pharisee. It was the prodigal who received the Father's love, not the good son. The good son couldn't—he was self-consumed.

Which is why we yield. Which is why we trust. Which is why we submit as Jesus to evil, because yielding yields life. Death is life's womb—we die to our own choices and opinions, in favor of others'.[28] Remember, he who saves his life will lose it. But he who loses his life for my sake, and for the kingdom, will find it—dead man walking.

If we don't sacrifice self, we can't call ourselves the Body of Christ. We have become mere table salt that has lost its flavor.

Jesus as Christ in love with a world enshrouded by evil came to destroy the shroud, to open the door to eternity and life and love. The Gospels aren't wrong just because they are dualistic. The battle is still one of evil against good, of Satan against God, of death against life. The promise is that we are already victors. The curse is that we still see as in a glass dimly. The hope is that we don't have to.

chapter six
stop fighting

If one were paying attention, one might suspect the Episcopal Church of falling into the generational abyss identified by Edwin Friedman in his seminal work, *Generation to Generation.* In short, Dr. Friedman suggested that succeeding generations of families and religious institutions naturally adopt the behavior patterns of previous generations, some good, some not so good, both functional and dysfunctional.

Some families—and we've all known one—are more comfortable fighting than living in peace. The Episcopal Church is just such a family.

We've fought for generations. We'be been fighting as far back as I can remember. Remember Bishop Pike? The 1979 Prayer Book? Ordaining Women? And now, the issue of Gay bishops and same sex blessings and marriages. The point isn't whether or not these fights are good, whether or not important issues are at stake. The point is the engagement itself—the morality of the engagement (how we fight), and the fact that we can't seem to *not* fight. Each fight or struggle seems to require a winner and a loser, a zero sum game.

I show you a more excellent way, Paul wrote.

Jesus both promised *and* warned, *you will know them by their fruit*. At the risk of over-simplifying and offering an incomplete list, Episcopal fruit as I see it is this:

(a) a beautiful spirituality among those willing to be engaged;

(b) a spirituality broad enough in expression to welcome a wide variety of people who have experienced Christ in a wide variety of ways (charismatic, evangelical, anglo-catholic, contemplative—all centered around the Eucharist);

(c) abject failure to challenge and infuse three-fourths of Episcopalians with a spirituality deeper than a once-a-month lip-service, or a "ChEaster" (Christmas/Easter) mentality;

(d) beautiful attempts and many successes at reaching out beyond our walls, for both social justice and societal change;

(e) red-faced embarrassment at the cutting edge word of the Gospel, its challenge, and its distinction from a 21st century America;

(f) too much fighting; and

(g) declining membership, due in-part to (b), (e) and (f) above.

Some of our fruit is tasty, while some is rotten. To use the parallel Scriptural metaphor, branches of our tree are barren.

Jesus cursed the barren fig tree, and it withered immediately (Mk. 11:12-14, 20-22; Matt. 21:18-22). He told the story about a barren fig tree given one additional year before being laid to the axe (Lk. 13:6). Fruit is crucial; it indicates the health of the organic system.

Perhaps we read Jesus' stories and aphorisms about fruit trees glibly, and imagine like the Pharisees that they apply only to others (Lk. 18:9-14). But, of course, we'd be wrong. Like I've said repeatedly, we're wrong regardless of which side of the present dispute we find ourselves. We're wrong because this is not a zero sum game. We're wrong because it is the whole tree, and not just a barren branch, that is afflicted. We're wrong because we're all in this together, as a whole, and not merely the sum of parts. We're wrong because it is *Our* Father, and not *My* Father, which art in heaven.

And we're made even more wrong because God has given us a magical and holy gift. What other Christian denomination pivots on worship and not doctrine? What other Christian denomination accommodates disparate thinkers around a common table? Certainly not Roman Catholic, and very few Protestant denominations.

And, we have received other gifts the world desperately seeks—only we don't seem to know it. The holy things of God, the very presence of God by the Holy Spirit, living and breathing in and through each of us, and all of us collectively. The gift of love, we are its ambry.

Just imagine, what if we *could* find the way forward, the way to disagree, love, and remain unified? Well, now, wouldn't that be something? And disparate factions coalescing around love—what a gift to the world that might be. For this to happen, change is in order.

Change means each of us must yield, must relinquish something. It means each of us must yield to the *other* among us. And, as any priest will tell you, breaking a church free from its Dr. Friedman-like generational curse is not just difficult, it is almost impossible.

Almost.

The earliest church had to change. Luke's tandem story of Jesus calming the storm and the Gerasenes demoniac reflect their struggle for change.

The evangelist, Luke, tells the Good News in two parts: The Gospel According to Luke and The Acts of the Apostles. Simple geography is crucial to Luke's story, the physical movement of Jesus and the Gospel from Galilee to Jerusalem. Jesus of Nazareth in Galilee (northern Israel, adjacent to the Sea of Galilee) chooses Galileans as disciples, and begins a three-part ministry. First, he heals and teaches in

Galilee (at the north), near and around the Sea. Second, he sets his face southward towards Jerusalem (Lk. 9:51), and he heals and teaches along the way. Third, he confronts the establishment and teaches in Jerusalem.

Acts, Part II of Luke's work, is all about the geographic progression of The Way (as it was called) from Jerusalem to the whole world. Salvation is not for the Jews alone, as they had suspected, but for all of humanity. Jesus as Messiah became Israel's gift to the world (see, e.g., *The Nunc Dimittis*, Lk. 2:29-32). Through Acts, Luke describes the fulfillment of the ages-old promise expressed throughout the Hebrew Scriptures in this regard.

Galilee to Jerusalem, Jerusalem to the world. Luke diverts from this geographic thesis only once, while still in Galilee, when Jesus implores his disciples, *Let's go to the other side of the Lake* (Lk. 8:22). The other side of the lake is present-day Jordan, which in Jesus' day, was Gentile territory, under Roman occupation. The disciples must have asked themselves, *Why would Jesus want to go there?*[29]

Peter, James and John are fishermen, and almost certainly can swim (see Jn. 21:4-8). Also, these fishermen would have battled storms before, so it is incredible that they would wake Jesus out of fear and (essentially) accuse him: *We are perishing!* (Lk. 8:22-25). Consider Mark's raw accusation: *Don't you care that we are perishing?* (Mk. 4:39). The real question is not whether Jesus cares or will calm the storm, but why are the disciples so afraid? They are afraid of the uncontrollable future. The storm is an incarnation of their fear. It represents the evil and unpredictability they are about to encounter on the other side. The storm thus becomes a portal to another place, a place of discomfort, a place of change. You encounter darkness when you are about to change.

Jesus, of course, calms the storm. The boat arrives at the opposite shore, and immediately (while one foot is in the boat, and the other on land, Lk. 8:26), Jesus is accosted by the Gerasenes demoniac. Is it actual demon possession, or is it mental illness? It doesn't matter; the existence of demons in this story is a red herring issue. You don't need to believe in demon possession in order to get Luke's point. Instead, all you need to do is agree that the disciples are venturing into a territory that for them is foreign, and because it is unclean, wholly evil. Or, because it is evil, wholly unclean.

This world is unclean and/or evil for four reasons: (1) Gentiles are generally unclean. (2) This man lives among tombs, contact with which makes one unclean (Nb. 19:16). (3) The demons are named *Legion*. This is a word-play, meaning both *Mob*, for there are so many, and a reference to the Roman Occupation. A legion was a group of Roman soldiers. The Roman occupation was, again, *unclean,* or evil. (4) Pigs.

Like I said, demon possession is a red herring issue. This story is about the disciples, and about

Jesus taking them against their will into a whole new world. The storm is a portal to change. The story is also about Jesus, and his identity. *Who is this man who even the wind and seas obey?*

The Disciples. Luke wrote Luke-Acts to a young church. Luke traveled with Paul, and thus Luke's intended audience was Paul's churches. Paul established churches outside of Israel in Gentile territory. These churches consisted of both Jew and Gentile. Galatia, Phillipi, Rome, and so on. Luke-Acts was thus written to both Jews and Gentiles, including Roman citizens (like Paul). This audience would have already known about the early conversion of the Church from a Jewish sect allowing only those Gentiles who converted to Judaism, to a Gentile sect whose roots were in Judaism. These believers understood change. They had heard the story of the Council at Jerusalem, of Peter and James and the elders deciding once and for all that Gentile converts need not observe Jewish purity laws or be circumcised. They would have heard the story of Peter's early vision, the one in which God says to Peter, *Call nothing God has made, unclean* (see Acts 10). Being Gentile was no longer *unclean*. Being Roman was no longer bad. In fact, Luke's intended audience would have known that salvation history, the presence of God through Israel, was not for the Jews primarily, but for them.

And now, hearing again this story of Jesus encountering a storm while crossing the lake to reach

Gentile (unclean) land occupied by unclean Romans to heal an unclean man by sending his uncleanness into unclean pigs, which then race into the same water that so frightened these Jewish fishermen— well, now, the irony is so obvious! Luke's audience would have laughed and cheered! They would have been an enthusiastic group of Young Republicans attending a JohnMcCain rally. They already knew the end of the story—that the *unclean* is no longer *unclean*. And the disciples in this story were foils, of a sort—there to make a point. Change.

The audience would have noted with some satisfaction the disciples' struggle, the storm, the change required for them to move from the comfortable and familiar side of the lake to the uncomfortable foreign side. Which is why they would have seen the storm as a portal, a metaphor for change. Change is tumultuous, fearful, and appears evil. Change is a dark storm, but demons are overcome through change. You find new life on the other side.

Jesus. In the final and great irony to this story, the de-possessed man naturally asks Jesus if he can follow. Jesus replies, *Go home and tell them all that God has done for you.* The man goes home, but rather than tell them all that God has done for him, the man tells them *all that Jesus has done for him* (Lk. 8:39). This play on words—from God to Jesus—is no accidental slip. It is Luke's answer to his earlier question, asked when Jesus calmed the storm: *Who is this man who even the wind and the seas obey?* (*para.* Lk. 8:25). Luke answered the question at the outset: the Son of God (Lk. 1:35), who exalts the lowly, fills the hungry, and sends the rich away empty-handed (Lk. 1:52, 53). God has not left the possessed man alone, and God has not left us alone! God with Jew, *and* God with Gentile. God with clean, God with unclean. All are accepted in Christ.

I can't help but believe that Jesus is taking the Episcopal Church to the other shore, through the storm. Forcing us to face our own fears, our own demons, our own sense of what is *unclean* and what is not. I don't mean this in the context of homosexuality. Homosexuality, and its acceptance or rejection, is worth discussing, as are all issues of faith, humanity, and morality. Indeed, becoming more tender, more human, may be the foreign shore to which Jesus is taking us. But our struggle is far deeper than the issue of Christian homosexuality. It has to do with our understanding of God and Jesus and Good News and one another. It has to do with our ability and inability to negotiate stormy waters of disagreement and debate. It has to do with zero sum game, and the concept that my gain is only balanced by your loss. Christianity is not a zero sum game. All can win.

And more importantly, our struggle has everything to do with the broader world in which we live, the world in which chaos and war and division thrive. Legion as a plethora of demons. In short, I am convinced that God's plan is to take us through the storm, to tame the demons of our division, for this purpose: so we can help the world tame its demons.

Which is why we *must* stop fighting. We must lay down the sword. Regardless of the repercussions.

We shouldn't be dividing over homosexuality, or over anything, for that matter. Not even Scriptural interpretation. Disagreeing, yes; dividing, no. Rather, we should be finding out how God might have us live together with diversity of opinion, with diversity of worship, with diversity of spiritualities. We are Anglicans, after all. Our gift is *via media*, not extremism.

As I've said, the world deeply longs for means, for a pathway to peace. The kingdom of God come to earth as it is in heaven is about peace. Emmanuel, God with us, the Prince of peace. This storm through which Jesus is leading us is but a radar blip on Weather.com—but it is necessary for us to navigate to lead us to the all-important other side, where our own fears and anxieties and prejudices can be cast as unclean pigs into the deep.

I hear the clarion call to good, old-fashioned repentance. Amendment of life. Turning from sin, the sin of division, the sin of failure to love, the sin of the Corinthians. From doing that which we ought not to have done, and not doing that which we ought to have done. And more practically, to turn our struggle from one about divisive issues (which must be discussed and debated absent ridiculous emotionalism and fear) to the more crucial issue of moving forward.

And that, in short, is my thesis. We have sinned, and there is no health in us. The very Body of Christ intended by Christ to take mission and gifts to the world is crouching over these gifts, plucking at them as one plucks a chicken. We're destroying the gifts of God, and at the end of the day, God in Christ won't allow that behavior to continue forever. We are in jeopardy of judgment—which, as I recall, begins in the household of God. It is better for us to judge ourselves, than to—again, as it is written—fall into the hands of the living God.

I pray it's not too late. And I pray we act. Or more to the point, I pray we stop acting—like children. Or, as I said at the beginning, pigs rolling around in our own slop. We are children of the Most High—not the pigs. The pigs end up in the water.

notes

1   There are two church organizations to split: the Anglican Communion, which, it appears, has already opened the door to eject the Episcopal Church; and the Episcopal Church, from which churches are fleeing and at least one diocese has left.

2   I use the word "activity" to mean, for example, disloyal behavior that, in heterosexual relationships is called, "adultery," or "cheating." I do not use "activity" to mean types of sexual acts.

3   I am betting we don't talk about these other "sins" because if we did, our churches might be as empty as England's!

4   For whatever reason, the person with nominal power, Archbishop Rowan Williams, seems to have very little real power, perhaps because he is choosing not to exercise his nominal power.

5   The text is ambiguous as to whose faith counts. Is it your faith, or is it the faith of Christ, that saves you?

6   Theissen, Gerd, *The Social Setting of Pauline Christianity* (*Essays on Corinth*), Schutz, J.H., transl., ed. (Philadelphia: Fortress Press, 1982), p. 72.

7   It should be noted that wisdom and knowledge were prized by the Corinthian culture—much like a progressive philosophy is prized in parts of our own culture. Paul does not dismiss wisdom and knowledge outright, but welcomes them as secondary to Christ, and then only when bound by love.

8   In response to an article I wrote for *The Living Church* in the Fall of 2006, one fellow wrote (in a letter to the editor) exactly this. Questioning the salvation and spirituality of the opponent is certainly a sad darkness formed in the heart of division. I have heard from progressives similar stuff: *the problem with the moral majority is that they are neither—moral nor the majority.* This rhetoric exposes a failure to trust and love.

9   This paragraph will make progressives bristle.

Certainly there is a time in history for groups and nations to make change by force—and maybe this is the time. I cannot help but wonder, however, if there might have been a better way. What if, for example, Bishop Robinson had been approved, and then he, along with other gays, moved to the podium at General Convention, and collectively withdrew his name? Some sort of passive nonresistance, to move the debate forward?

10 MacDonald, George. *Unspoken Sermons*, Series One, Alexander Strahan, London, 1867.

11 My friend Betsy Rosen is worried that I sound anti-Jewish and anti-Israel, here. She wrote to me: "Surely [you don't mean Israel was barren or fruitless]! If Israel had been fruitless then, it would be fruitless now, and that is a blasphemy! Unless you are a supercessionist, and believe that God entirely transferred his imprimatur from Judaism to Christianity as we know it. I believe that something much more mysterious and incomplete happened/continues to happen. Why has Judaism not died out, like so many hundreds of other religions? Could it be because it still has something to teach us, something that "the church" forgot to pick up and take with it as it veered off from Judaism, somewhere there in the midst of very human quarrels? Just a thought."

Betsy is quite correct, and I do not believe nor

do I mean to suggest that Israel (either nominally or as a group of individual Jewish people) is or was fruitless. My point here is to suggest that Matthew arranged a sequence of encounters, between Jesus and the authorities, into Holy Week as a judgment on Israel (its leaders) in favor of the new Church. He employed dramatic license to make his point, a type of hyperbole through story development. Unfortunately, the Church all too often has interpreted the Gospels as meaning that God has rejected Israel and all Jews. We (the Christian Church universal) could have saved ourselves a sordid history and the potential if not actual judgment of God had we not assumed God rejected Israel and its people in favor of the Church. In fact, Paul proves exactly the opposite, when he writes in Romans that all Jews will be saved. See Romans 11:26.

I, however, want to be faithful to Matthew's writing. The early Church wrestled with the role of Israel and the Jews. Matthew is wrestling, here, but his overarching theme is not the rejection of Israel or the Jews, but that God is forming a new community (the Church) because the old community (Israel, acting through its religious leaders) failed to act as God needed for the salvation of the world. I explain all of this to make the point that the Lord's Prayer is a prayer for and about the Church; it is about Church unity, as far as Matthew is concerned—a unity prayer, a binding agent. And so, if you have something against your brother or sister, leave the altar, and go, be reconciled, and then come offer your gift. Thank you, Betsy!

12 The religious leaders ask Jesus by whose authority he acts. He will tell them, he says, if they can tell him where John the Baptist received his authority, from God or man. This trap confounds and embarrasses them, and Jesus' message becomes obvious: their authority is baseless. See Matt. 21:23-27.

13 Jesus distinguishes the religious leaders from the people (and Jerusalem) when he weeps over Jerusalem at the end of the Woes (see below)—*Jerusalem, Jerusalem, you that kill the prophet...* (Matt. 22:37-39).

14 At this point, Jesus impeaches the religious leaders by his list of woes (*Woe to you, Scribes and Pharisees, hypocrites!*—see Matt. 23:13-36).

15 Matthew is the only Evangelist to use the actual word, *church*. See Matt. 16:18, 18:17.

16 Moses and Jesus are both threatened as toddlers with death—Moses, by Pharoah who killed all boys under two, and Jesus, by Herod, who likewise killed all boys under two. Both children are saved miraculously by God's intervention, and both children are raised in Egypt. Jesus becomes Moses in his polemic against the Jewish leaders, as though against Pharoah, Jesus, like Moses,

ascends the "Mount," that is, *goes up a hill*, to issue the law. Both Moses and Jesus turn General Electric white by transfiguration, so white as to blind others.

17 Often after I receive a distress telephone call, I hang-up, pause, lay my hand on the phone, and pray for the person who is the subject of the call. If I don't pray with words, I offer silence.

18 When I jog in a solitary place, the rhythm of my feet on the pavement becomes a cadence much like the repetition of a word in Centering Prayer. I sense the presence of God in the solitude, and our union becomes prayer.

19 If I may be so bold, the Eucharist is actually a form of intercourse, of great intimacy between God and the Church, in which each gives itself completely to the other in vulnerability. Each takes what he or she has received from the other, and then gives it back, changed, improved. God receives the elements from us, representations of our life and our labor, plus the cash offering (representing the same). Upon blessing, upon transformation, God returns them to us in the form of life, the body and blood of our Lord. We receive life, and the building blocks to create bread, wine and money, we bless them with labor and time, return them to God, who then gives them back to us in the form of eternity—the body and blood of Christ.

20 The reason the rubrics call for the priest to leave the offering of money on the altar table is because the money, too, represents our life and our labor given to the Lord—and, in this day, is more representative than bread and wine purchased by the Altar Guild.

21 I used to hear Christians declare, *I have to love you; I don't have to like you.* I would argue that Christ-love requires *like*, not of behavior, but of person. Isn't that the rub of the command? As one of my mentors used to say, *If it were easy, everybody'd do it*—which is quite similar, when you think about it, to Jesus' statement to love enemies. Even the heathen, after all, love those who love them back. Where is the value in that?

22 If I didn't know any better, I'd declare that God isn't answering prayer—for this prayer certainly seems unanswered.

23 Suggesting urgency.

24 Obviously, a person has no control over whether another will choose to be reconciled with him or her.

25 Buechner, Frederick, *Wishful Thinking*, (San Francisco: HarperCollins, 1993), p. 108.

26 Referring to God as "it" denudes God of personhood, which seems to me to be a much greater mistake than a politically incorrect gender.

27 The four Gospels are decidedly dualistic. Good battles against evil. Elaine Pagels ties the dualism to the existence of war, either of ongoing war in the case of Mark, or of recent war, as in the case of the other three Gospels. See generally, Pagels, Elaine, *The Origin of Satan*, chapter 1 (NY: Vintage Books, 1995).

Christians often ignore the presence of angels and demons in the Gospels, but angels and demons, good and evil, help explain why God would allow death and destruction in the human drama. The political situation in Israel at the time reflects the battle of the heavens, of God against Satan, of good against evil. Mark, if not all of the Evangelists, claim an eschatological victory, a future victory of God over Satan, as the explanation for the present and disastrous plight of humanity. See Pagels, p. 13.

In fact, Mark invites Satan into the story of the Good News at the outset. Jesus is baptized, the voice of the Father affirms him, and the Spirit (of God) drives Jesus into the wilderness to contend with Satan (Mark 1:13). Jesus contends with Satan not only in the wilderness, but throughout the Gospel, as he encounters soul after soul bound and riddled with the physical infirmity of evil (see, e.g., Mark 1:23-27).

Jesus shockingly calls his most loyal disciple "Satan" when Peter tempts him to avoid the cross (Mark 8:33). Jesus responds by telling Peter to take up his cross—which is the God's calling to all of us (Mark 8:34). Those who save their life will lose it; those who lose theirs, will save it. You must, you absolutely must, lay down your life. The paradox: the only live Christian is a dead one.

It is no accident that darkness came over the land for three hours, beginning at noon (Mark 15:33). God as God forsook the crucified Son, abandoning him fully to death and evil. *Eloi, Eloi, lema sabacthani* (Mark 15:34). Jesus finally breathed his last, whereupon the centurion outsider—the only person in Mark's Gospel to fully recognize Jesus as the Son of God—proclaims, *Truly this man was God's Son* (Mark 15:39).

For Mark and the other Gospel writers, the Jewish establishment against whom Jesus seems to rail is a straw man. It is evil, it is the devil, it is the darkness who is waging war against God; the religious leaders have become evil's pawns.

28 You can have an opinion—even a strong opinion—as to any given issue in the church and still yield to others. We aren't called to be people without opinion; we are called to be humble people with opinion.

28 Later, Luke's Jesus travels straight through Samaria. Samaria is not Jewish territory and the Samaritans and Jews hated each other. Whereas the Jews believed God was to be worshipped in

Jerusalem, the Samaritans believed God was properly worshipped on Mt. Gerizim. Taking the disciples through Samaria is another unanticipated travel moment that surprised them—but this little journey into Gentile territory across the Sea of Galilee was the first.